AF428227

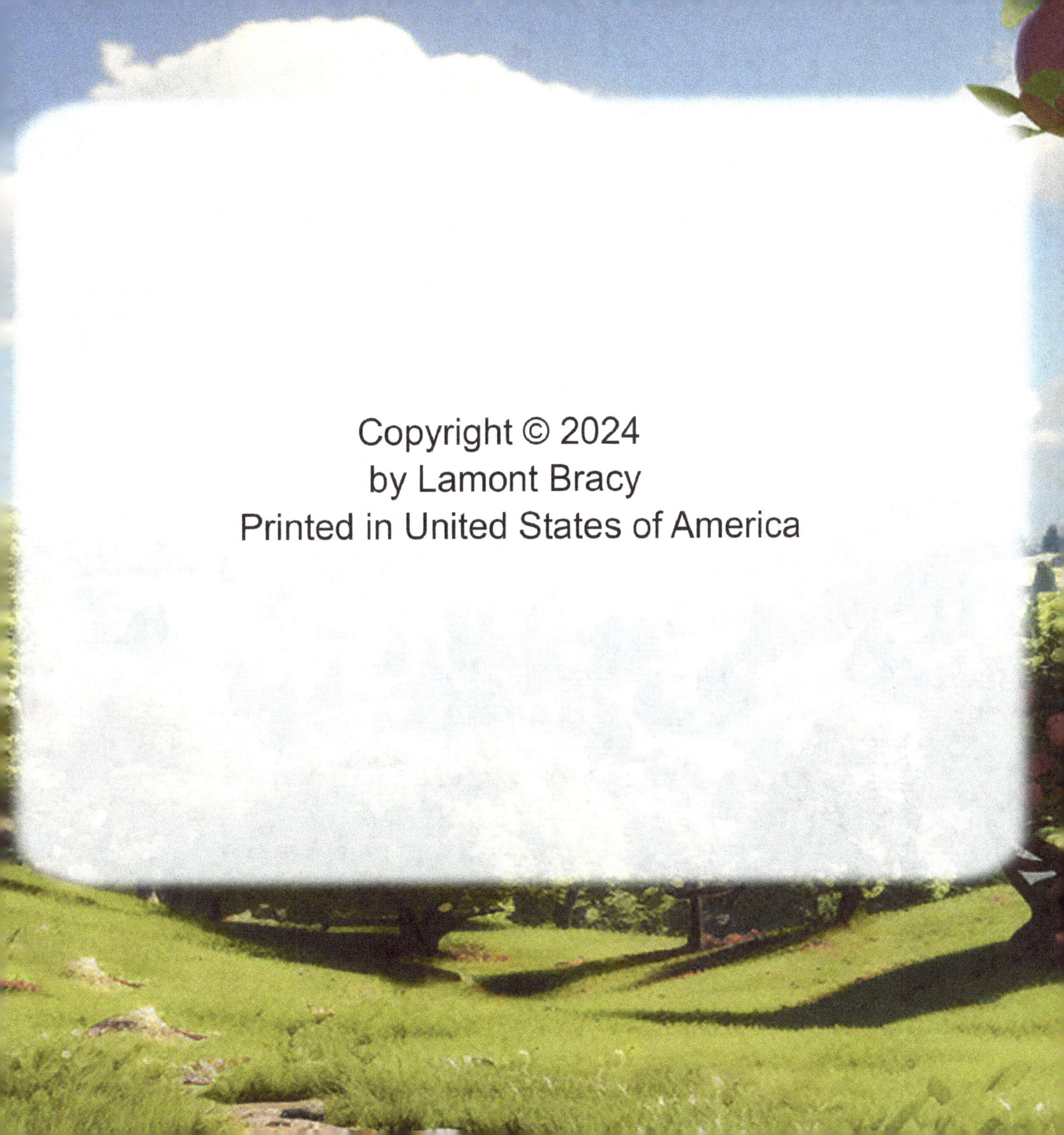

Copyright © 2024
by Lamont Bracy
Printed in United States of America

Hello, my name is Elliana.
I like math. Do you like math?

Do you like oranges and apples?
I also like oranges and apples.

I like to Add and Subtract oranges and apples. Do you like to add and subtract?
Let's Add Apples (+)

Elliana has 1 apple, and her sister Chanel gives her 1 apple. How many apples does Elliana have?
That's Correct!
Elliana now has 2 apples.
(1+1=2)

Elliana has 2 apples in her basket, if Chanel gives her 2 apples, how many apples do Elliana have in her basket?
That's right, Elliana now has 4 apples in her basket.
(2+2=4)
4 apples

You are good at counting apples!
Let's ADD more apples.

Elliana picked 3 apples from the apple tree. Chanel also picked 3 apples from the tree. The girls place their apples in the basket. How many apples
That's Right, the girls now have 6 apples in the basket.
(3+3=6)
6 apples
9

Elliana and Chanel love to pick apples.
2
9

Elliana wants more apples. The girls use a ladder to reach the apples. Chanel picks 4 apples and Elliana picks 4 apples. How many apples are in the basket?
If you said 8 apples, you are correct! Great Job
(4+4=8)
8 apples are in the basket.

Let's Subtract (−) Oranges!!
🍊🍊 − 🍊 = 1

After leaving the apple orchard, the girls visit the orange grove with their basket. Elliana and Chanel pick oranges from the large trees.

The girls place the oranges in the basket, but the basket is too heavy. Elliana and Chanel must remove some of the oranges from the basket.

Elliana and Chanel have picked 6 oranges. Chanel takes 1 orange from the basket. How many oranges are in the basket?
That is correct, there are 5 oranges left in the basket.
(6-1=5)

Elliana and Chanel's basket is still too heavy. The girls must remove oranges to carry the basket.

After a long day of picking oranges and apples, the girls decide to only keep the two oranges left in the basket.

Counting using addition and subtraction is fun! Elliana and Chanel love to Add and Subtract.

Special Thanks

Thanks My precious granddaughters, Chanel and Elliana. To my daughters, Elizabeth, and Chantel, keep striving for greatness. My parents, George T. Bracy Jr. and Emily Bracy. The entire Bracy, Butts, Peterson, and Scott family, thank YOU! My amazing team, Thank You for the beautiful artwork and illustrations. Michael Stinson ESQ at World Premiere Agency - You Rock! To my fans and supporters... I thank you for every act of kindness, donations, and support.

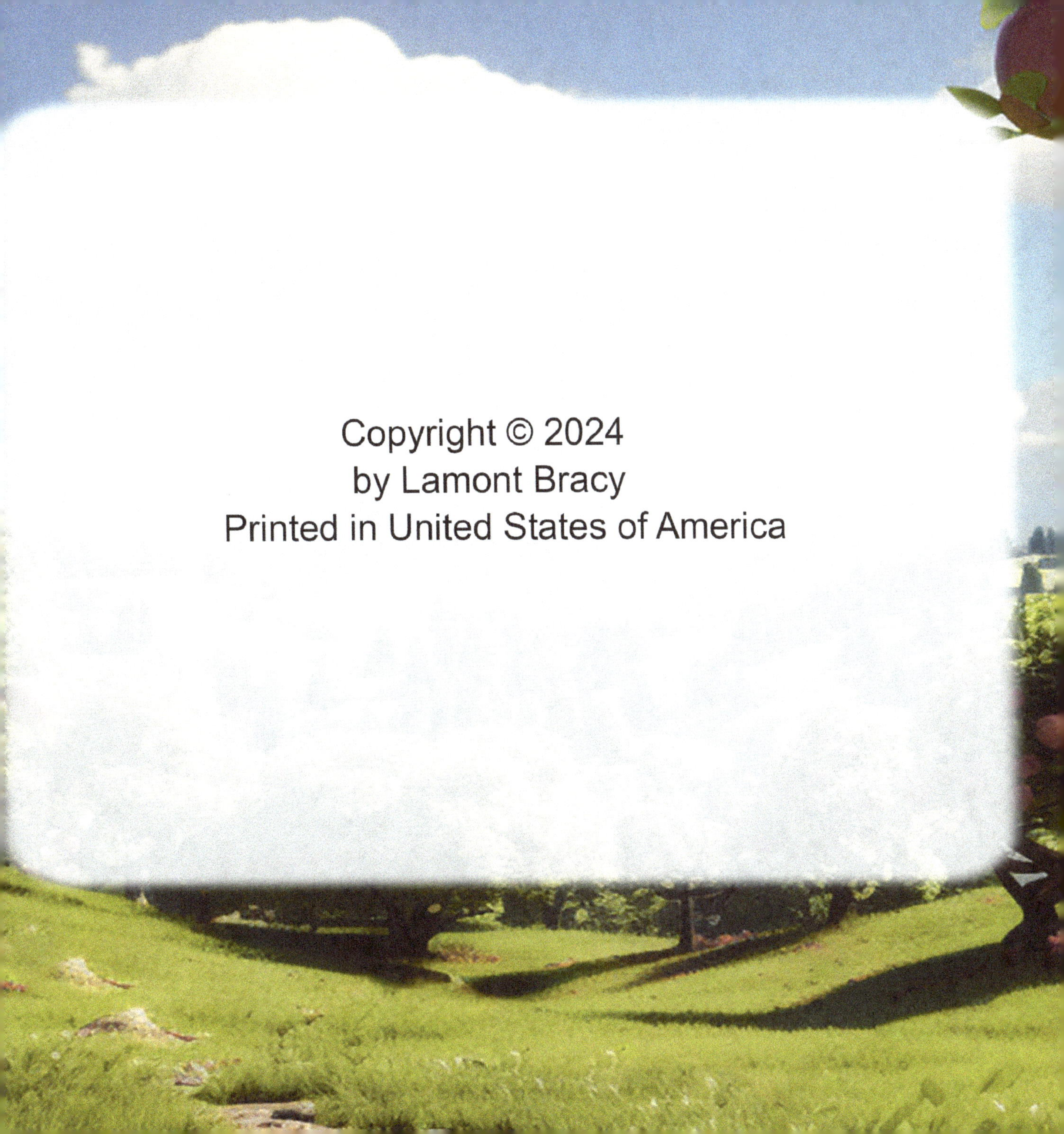